Sounds Write

Published by Sounds Write 2024

Copyright © James C. Baskett 2024

All rights reserved.
No part of this publication may be reproduced, stored in a retrieval system, or transmitted, in any form or by any means, without the prior permission in writing of the copyright owner, nor be otherwise circulated in any form of binding or cover other than that in which it is published and without similar condition including this condition being imposed on the subsequent purchaser.

ISBN 978-1-902511-18-4

Sounds Write
www.soundswrite.uk

Know Your Bass
By James Baskett

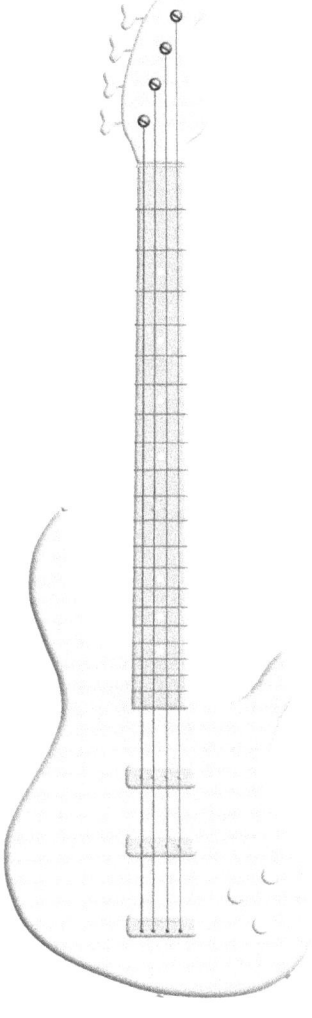

Patterns For Free Bass Playing

Contents

Introduction	1.
Parts of The Bass Guitar	2.
Finding Your Way Around The Fretboard	3.
Open Strings & Tuning	4.
Tuning The Bass Without a Tuner	6.
Finding The Right Note	7.
All The Notes – The Chromatic Scale	8.
Notes Along The String – Naturals & Sharps	9.
Notes Along The String – Naturals & Flats	10.
Notes Across The Strings	11.
Finding Your Way Around the Bass	12.
The Major Scale	13.
Playing The Major Scale	14.
The Minor Scale	16.
Playing The Minor Scale	18.
Common Intervals	20.
The Octave (8th)	24.
Common Chords and How to Find Them	25.
Notes Within a Chord	26.
The Pentatonic Scale	28.
Blues Notes & Passing Notes	29.
Playing The Minor Pentatonic Scale	30.
The Blues Scale	32.
Playing The Blues Scale	33.
TAB	34.
Scale Position	44.
Notes	54.

Introduction

When you know a house it becomes a home and you can find your way around, even with the lights off. You know where things are kept and don't have to think about where to find the bathroom. It is the same with a bass. When you first pick it up, it will feel cumbersome and awkward. Finding your first notes will take time and each riff and bass part will need to be learnt individually. Once you know your bass, you can find your way around it with your eyes closed and notes and progressions flow together. Many bassists get stuck learning parts and finding notes because they never learn the patterns that enable free movement and fluidity.

This guide is designed to liberate the bassist and to enable them to move intuitively around the fretboard, finding the note they want to make the riff they desire. Learning the patterns within will enable you to improvise and play with others with confidence, even when you are thrown a bass solo out of the blue - it does happen! It will also enable you to create your own bass parts, solos and enjoy getting creative with your bass guitar. As you get to know the bass and the patterns that make it, the bass guitar will become more an extension of your own body than a tool you are using and your fingers will move intrinsically, finding their own way to the notes you want to play.

I hope this guide will give you all the tools you need to truly enjoy your bass guitar and the confidence to play, jam and improvise – and even perform.

Parts of The Bass Guitar

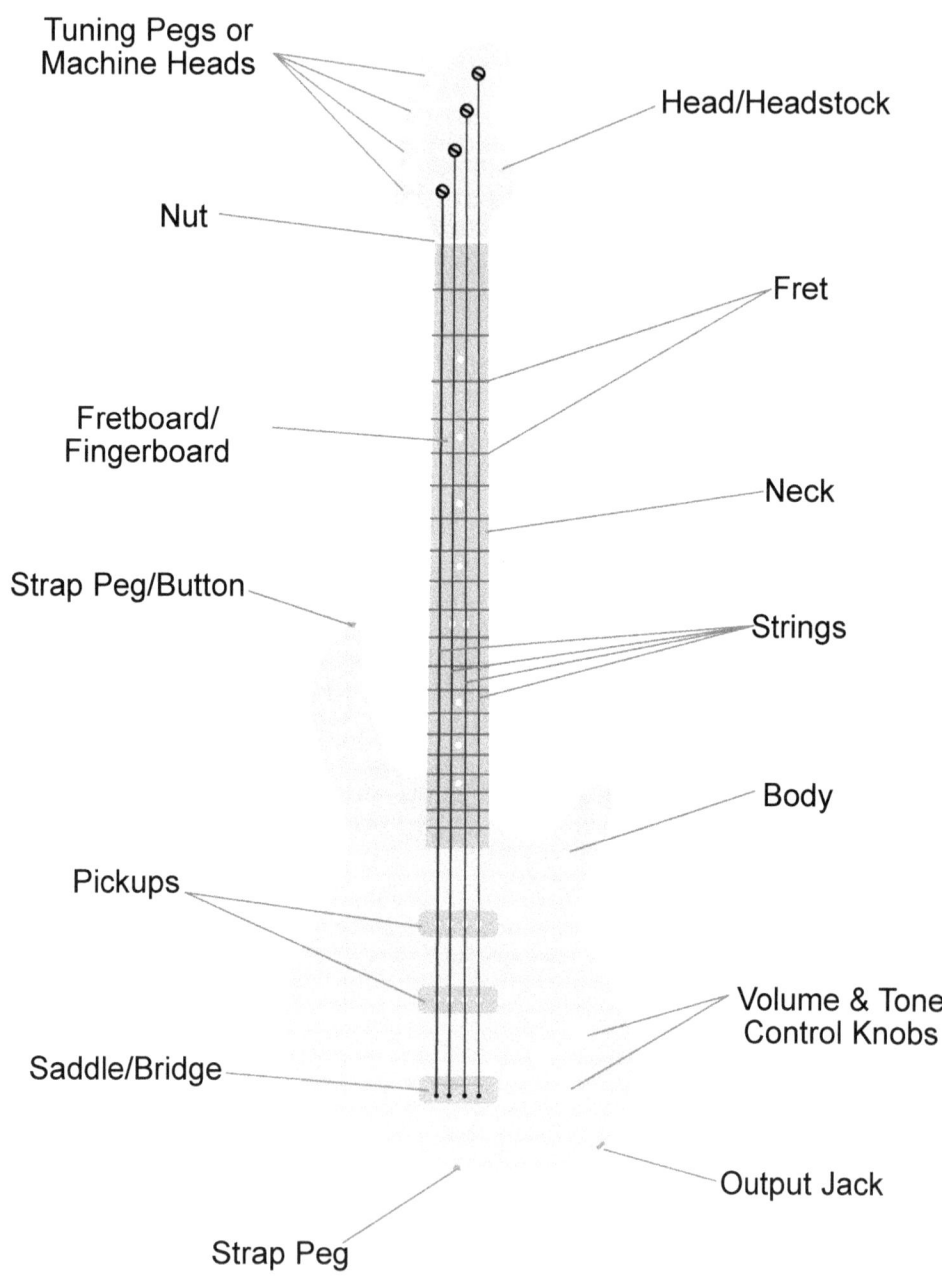

Finding Your Way Around The Fretboard

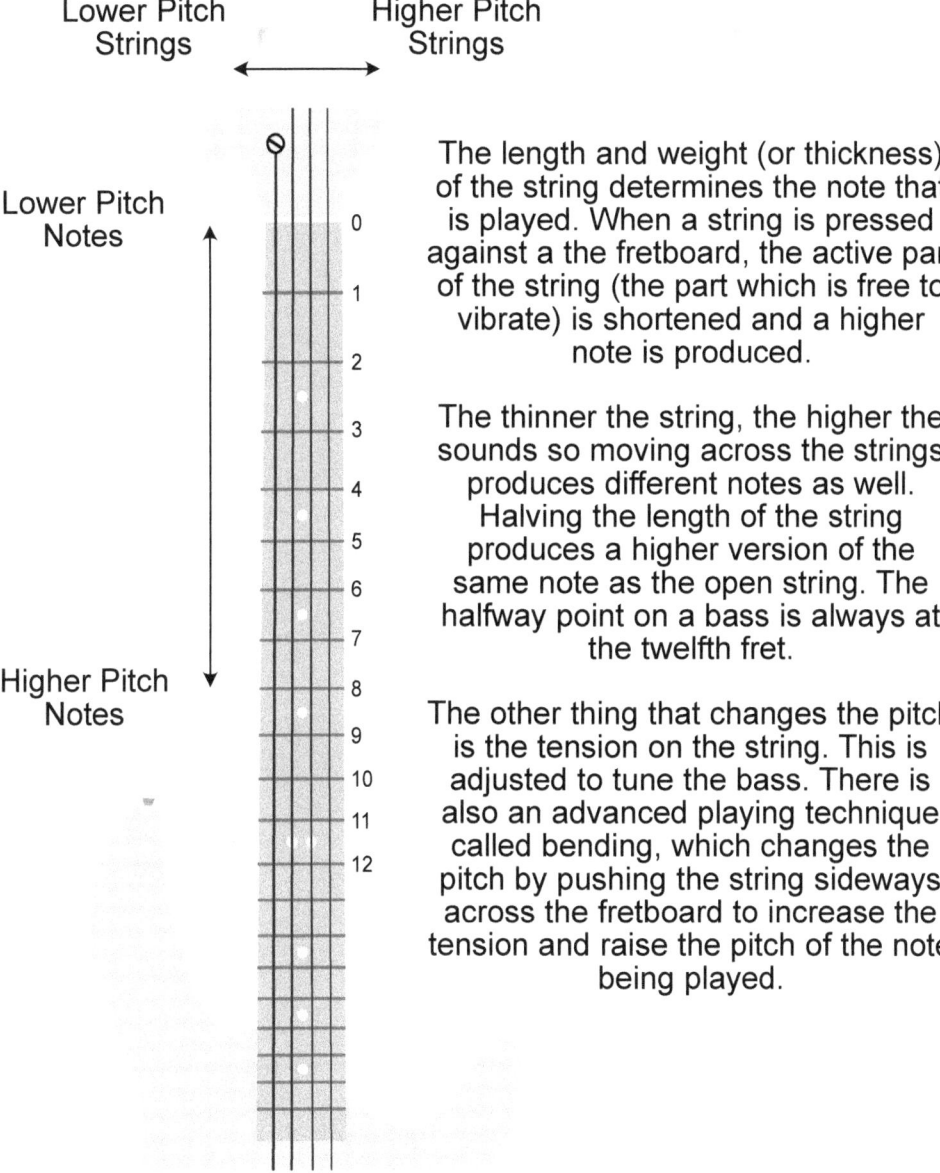

The length and weight (or thickness) of the string determines the note that is played. When a string is pressed against a the fretboard, the active part of the string (the part which is free to vibrate) is shortened and a higher note is produced.

The thinner the string, the higher the sounds so moving across the strings produces different notes as well. Halving the length of the string produces a higher version of the same note as the open string. The halfway point on a bass is always at the twelfth fret.

The other thing that changes the pitch is the tension on the string. This is adjusted to tune the bass. There is also an advanced playing technique called bending, which changes the pitch by pushing the string sideways across the fretboard to increase the tension and raise the pitch of the note being played.

Open Strings & Tuning

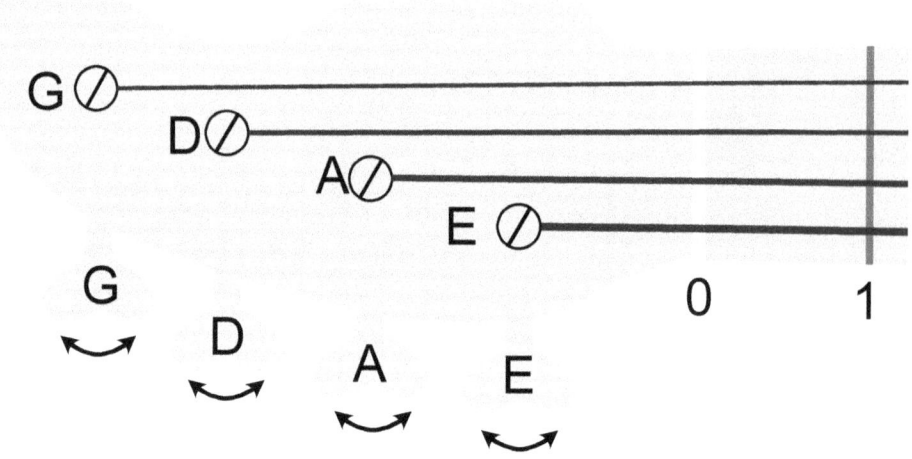

The strings on a standard 4-string bass are arranged E, A, D, G with the lowest in pitch being the E string.

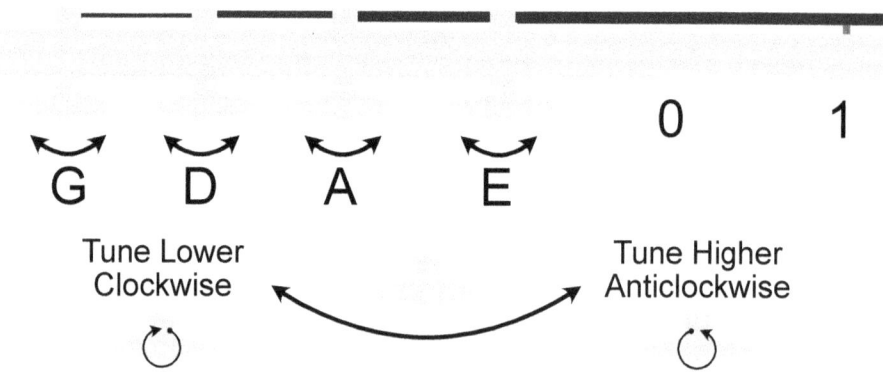

Tune Lower Clockwise

Tune Higher Anticlockwise

To tune the bass, turn the tuning peg either clockwise to go lower or anticlockwise to go higher until you achieve the note you want. If your bass has been set up incorrectly, you may find clockwise makes it higher and anticlockwise makes it lower. You can correct this by restringing it or just remember to go the other way.

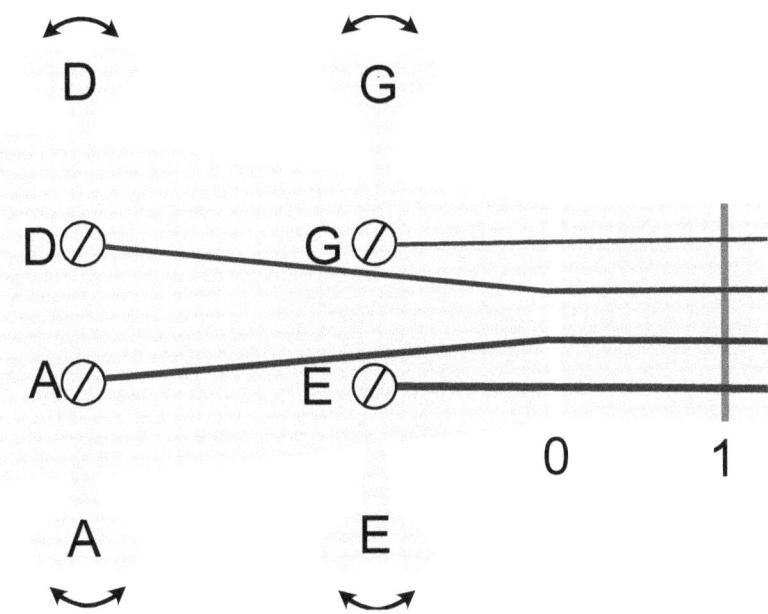

When basses are made with the tuning pegs on opposite sides of the head, we still tune the bass in exactly the same way. However, the pegs on the lower side of the head (D & G) need to be turned in the opposite direction when playing the bass and working from above. You will be able to hear whether or not you are tuning in the right direction when you check your note and will be able to adjust as necessary.

Tuning The Bass Without a Tuner

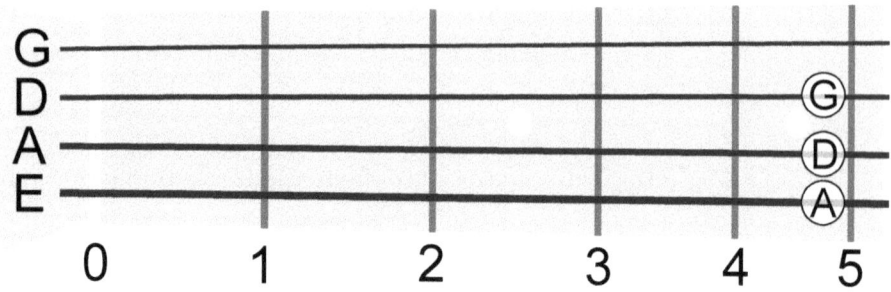

If you don't have a tuner you may need to tune the bass to itself or to other instruments in the band. First of all ask someone to give you a low E and adjust the corresponding tuning peg until you have the same pitch. Once you have tuned the E string, you can tune the next string, A, using the fifth fret on the E string.

Place your finger just behind the fifth fret on the E string and press down firmly. Play the E string and then the A string and adjust the tuning peg for the A string until it is the same pitch as the fifth fret on the E string. Keep checking the two strings until they sound the same.

Once the A string is tuned you can do the same to tune the D and G strings. Placing your finger in the fifth fret on the A string produces a D and placing your finger on the fifth fret of the D string produces a G.

Finding The Right Note

Each fret is positioned on the fretboard to give the next note along the string. Being able to find the right note is essential when playing along to music or with others.

The history of how notes got their names is long and complicated, however, most western music consists of seven different notes which repeat in higher and higher octaves. Together these notes are called a key and when arranged in an ascending or descending pattern they are referred to as a scale. In their most basic form these notes are labelled from A to G. These are 'natural' notes and in modern music are the notes which make up the key of C major.

Natural Notes

The C Major Scale

There are several different keys and scales, each starting on a different note, and C major is the only major scale which uses only natural notes. Western music names 12 notes and all other scales require notes which sit in between the natural notes. We refer to these as sharps and flats where sharp means higher than the natural and flat means lower that the natural. We use symbols to indicate whether a note is sharp, natural or flat.

Sharp	Natural	Flat
♯	♮	♭

When no symbol is written, the note is assumed to be natural.

All The Notes – The Chromatic Scale

All twelve notes used in western music can be written as either a combination of naturals and sharps or naturals and flats. For example, the note A sharp (A#) which is A but a little higher is the same note as B flat (Bb) or B but a little lower.

All twelve notes are written below first as a combination of naturals and sharps and then as naturals and flats.

Natural & Sharps

Naturals & Flats

When all twelve notes are arranged like this we call it a chromatic scale and the interval between each note is called a semitone (half a tone). If we combine sharps and flats together it is easy to see that some notes have two names.

Natural, Sharps & Flats

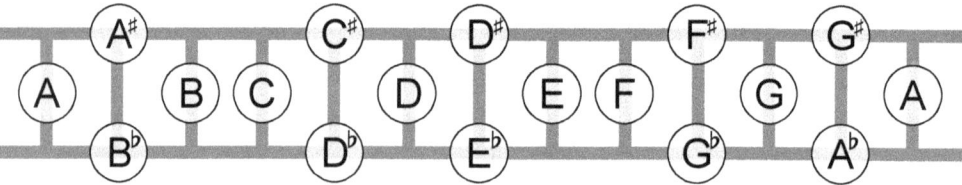

You will notice that not all natural notes have a sharp or flat between them. This is because the seven natural notes are the notes in the C major scale and a scale uses a combination of semitone and full tone intervals. For example, there is a full tone between an A and a B so A# or Bb sits in the gap but there is only a semitone between B and C so there is no space for another note between these two notes.

Notes Along a String – Naturals & Sharps

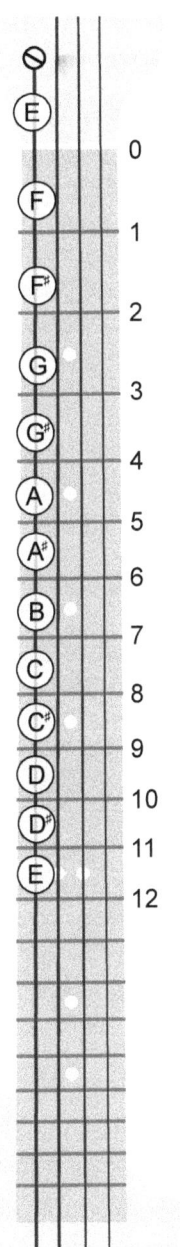

To find a note on a string, simply start with the note of the open string (the sound you get when plucking the string with no fingers pressed down). Locate that note in the sequence of Naturals & Sharps or Naturals & Flats and count along the frets with each fret giving you the next note in the sequence.

Here we start on the E string so the note of the open string is E. We find E in our chromatic sequence of notes and count along the string to find the note for each fret. Always place your finger just behind the fret to get the best sound and round your finger so that you are pressing with your finger tip rather than the pad of your finger - this will help you not to touch other strings while playing and will increase your finger speed with practice.

Note the white dots on frets 3, 5, 7 & 9 and the double white dot on fret 12. These will help you find the fret you want quickly and easily.

Notes Along a String – Naturals & Flats

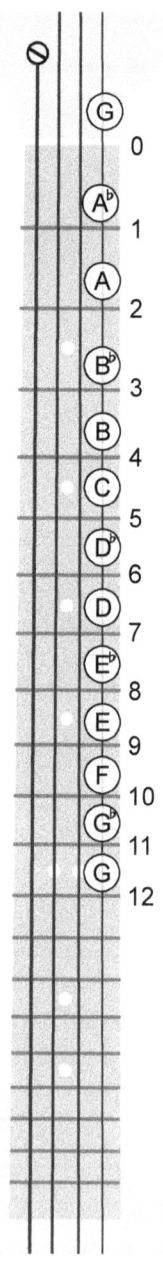

Here we start on the G string so the note of the open string is G. We find G in our chromatic sequence and count along the string to find the note for each fret. Whether you use sharps or flats, the process is exactly the same.

Your fretboard will have dots on it on the fifth, seventh, ninth and twelfth fret. These will help you find your way around the fretboard. Some basses also have a dot on the third fret.

You will notice that the note on the twelfth fret is the same as your open string. This is the halfway point on the string and the point at which the pattern starts again. It is called an octave. You can continue beyond the twelfth fret using the same pattern so the thirteenth and fourteenth frets are Ab and A respectively.

Notes Across The Strings

When working across the strings the same principle applies. Starting from the open string count along the string in the chromatic sequence of either sharps or flats. You will notice that the fifth fret is the same note as the open string above so here we move up a string and continue the sequence.

Naturals & Sharps

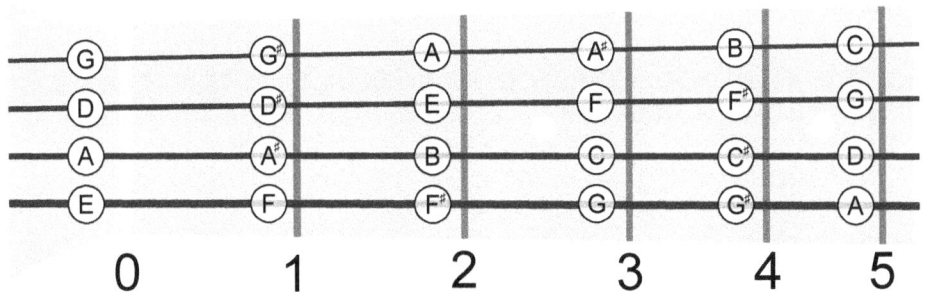

Naturals & Flats

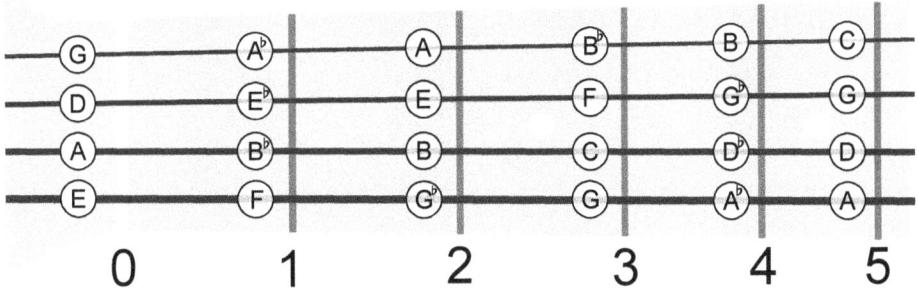

You can find the octaves across the strings by finding where the same note next appears. For example: fret 1 one the E string is an F. We find the next F on fret 3 of the D string. This is an octave interval. You will see that this interval is always the same: forward two frets and up two strings. This is one of the patterns that will help us to find our way around the bass guitar. We will look at more of these when we look at scales in the next section.

Finding Your Way Around The Bass

The easiest way to find your way around the fretboard on the bass is to learn patterns which repeat. We have already found that the note of the open string repeats at the half way point on the string on the twelfth fret and that we can find the same note on a different string by moving two frets forward and two strings up. Both of these movements take us up an octave and into the next repeat of the same pattern of chromatic notes.

We also discovered that most western music used seven different notes on repeat in different sequences and this gives us a scale pattern or a key. On the bass, the scale pattern is the same for every key (different set of notes). To get a different key, we just have to start the pattern in a different place. Therefore, scales are one of the most useful patterns to learn to help navigate the fretboard and to give us the basis for creating bass parts and improvising solos.

To help build consistency when learning the patterns, we number the fingers one to four.

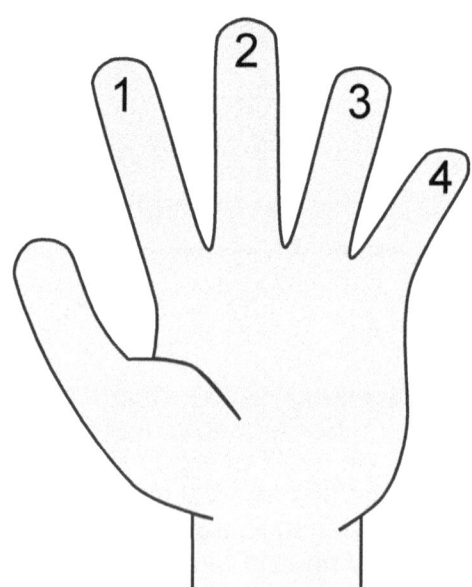

The Major Scale

The major scale is the 'happy' or 'joyous' scale and can start on any note (naturals, sharps or flats) but always uses the same pattern of tone and semitone intervals between the notes. Each note in the scale is referred to as a degree and degrees are numbered from 1st to 8th where the 8th is a higher version of the first degree and is called the octave. It is also the first note of the next repeat of the pattern.

A major scale - tone and semitone pattern

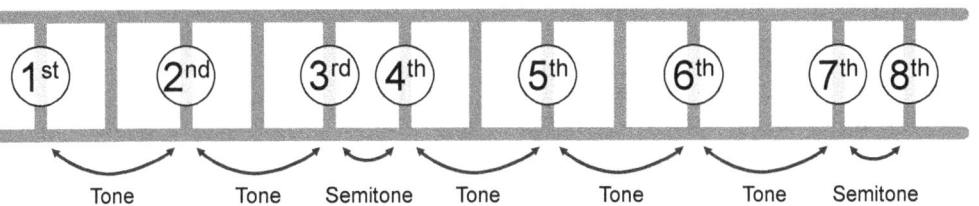

This translates onto the bass along the string as:

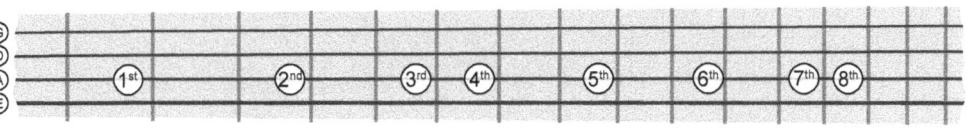

N.B. The frets are not numbered because this pattern can start on any fret on any string.

and translates across the strings as:

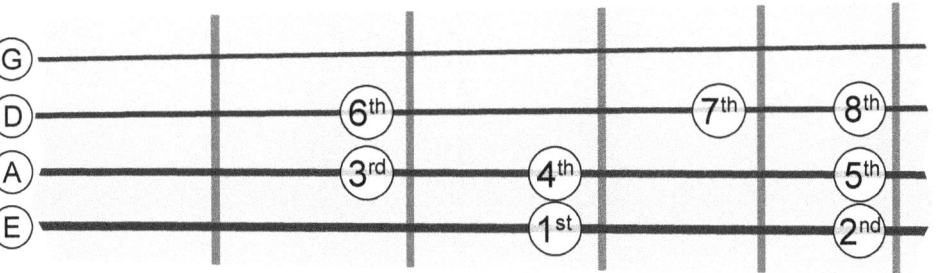

N.B. The frets are not numbered because this pattern can start on any fret on the E or A string.

Playing The Major Scale

To play the major scale, select a fret on either the E or A string and place your second finger on it. The note of this fret is the key of the scale. For example, starting with the second finger on the third fret of the E string gives the note G and the scale of G major.

The diagram below shows the scale pattern with fingering numbers. Position your hand around the chosen fret and imagine a block of four frets, one per finger. Play the ascending scale by starting with the lowest string and playing left to right along the string before moving up to the next string. The descending scale starts with the highest note and works downward, right to left before moving down a string and continuing right to left. Degrees in the scale are numbered in superscript above the fingering number.

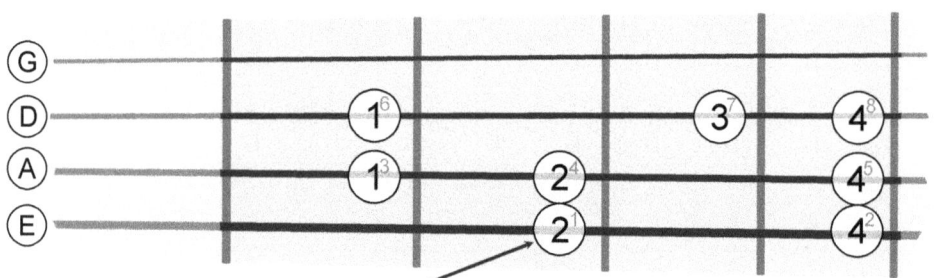

N.B. The frets are not numbered because this pattern can start on any fret on the E or A string.

Starting Note Ascending Scale

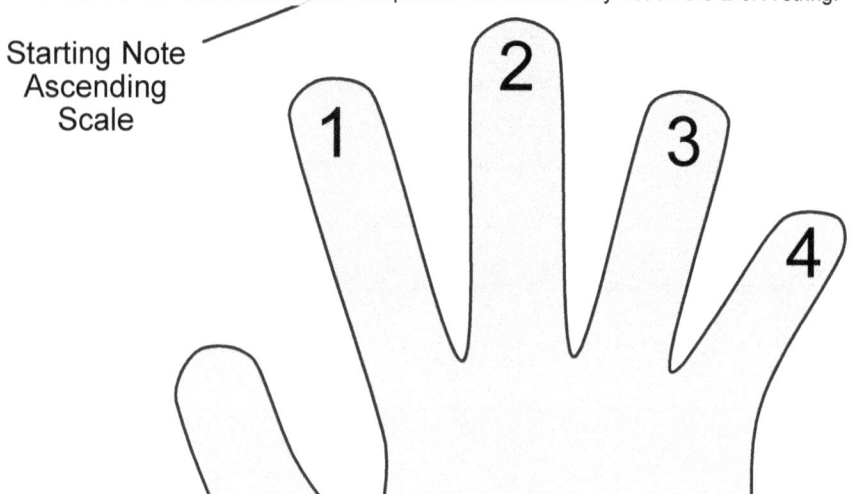

This is the same pattern starting on the A string:

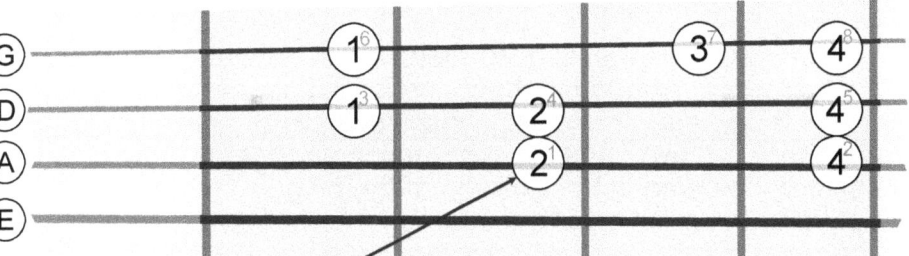

N.B. The frets are not numbered because this pattern can start on any fret on the E or A string.

Starting Note Ascending Scale

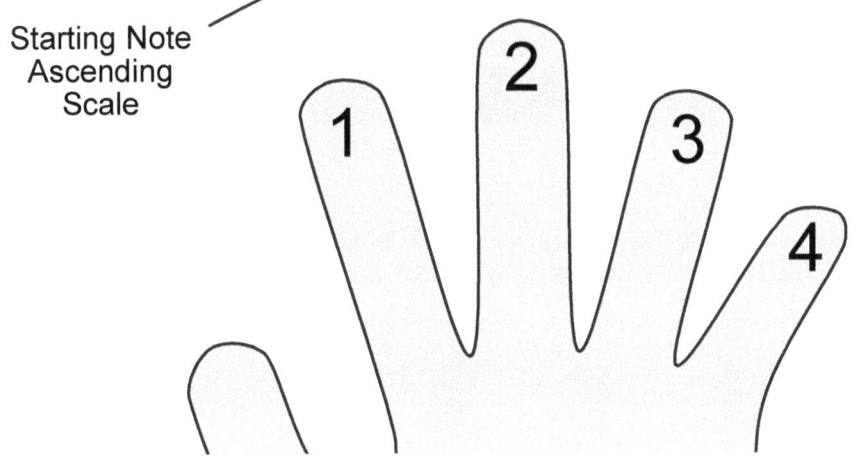

To start with, playing with one finger per fret may feel like a big stretch and the little finger may feel very awkward, however, this is a skill worth persevering with because it will make it easy to navigate the fretboard, create bass parts and improvise solos. Also, being able to use all four fingers greatly increases playing speed and dramatically reduces the amount the bassist needs to move up and down the fretboard to find notes.

The frets at the higher end on the bass are closer together. If you are struggling with the stretches, start the scale on the A string further down the fretboard and work back towards the head as your hands get used to this new position.

The Minor Scale

The minor scale is the 'sad' or 'melancholic' scale and can also start on any note (naturals, sharps or flats). Like the major scale it also has 8 degrees, however, in classical music, unlike the major scale, there are two variants, a harmonic and melodic minor with the difference being in the position of the 6th and 7th degrees. The adaption to the position of the 6th degree is very seldom used so, for our purposes, we will combine these two scales with an optional variation in the position of the 7th degree. All scales and patterns, once learned, are there to guide but not limit the bassist; everything can be adapted if by adapting it you get the sound you actually want. The degrees are numbered 1st to 8th where the 8th is again a higher repeat of the 1st degree and the first note of the next repeating pattern.

A harmonic minor scale - tone and semitone pattern

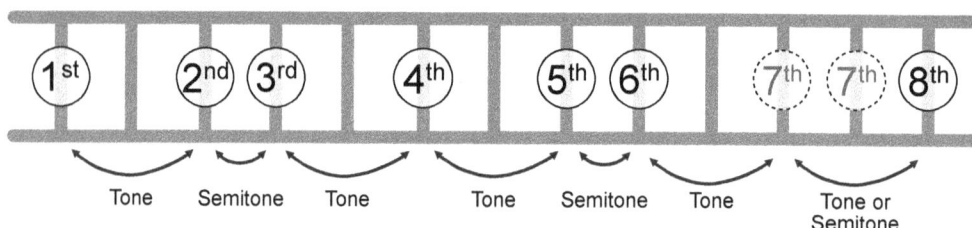

This translates onto the bass along the string as:

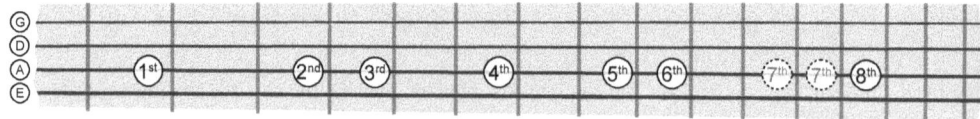

N.B. The frets are not numbered because this pattern can start on any fret on any string.

Our minor scale again fits into a nice four fret block and translates across the strings as:

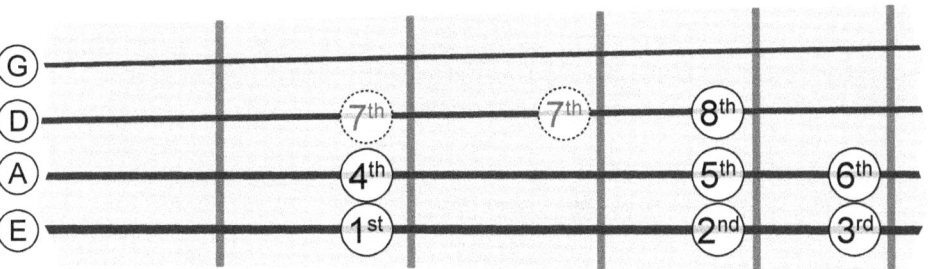

N.B. The frets are not numbered because this pattern can start on any fret on the E or A string.

When playing the scale, chose which position you wish to use for the 7th degree. It would be unusual to play both but, again as these scales are intended to guide rather than limit the bassist, there is no rule to say how you should use the scales.

Playing The Minor Scale

To play the minor scale, select a fret on either the E or A string and place your first finger on it. The note of this fret is the key of the scale. For example, starting with the first finger on the fifth fret of the E string produces the note A and the scale of A minor.

The diagram below shows the scale pattern with fingering numbers. Position your hand around the chosen fret and imagine a block of four frets, one per finger. Play the ascending scale by starting with the lowest string and playing left to right from the lowest note to the highest note along the string before moving up to the next string and doing the same. The descending scale starts with the highest note and works downward, right to left before moving down a string and continuing right to left. Degrees in the scale are numbered in superscript above the fingering number.

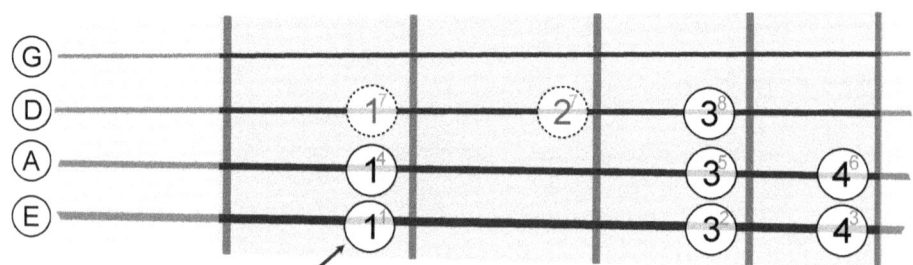

N.B. The frets are not numbered because this pattern can start on any fret on the E or A string.

Starting Note Ascending Scale

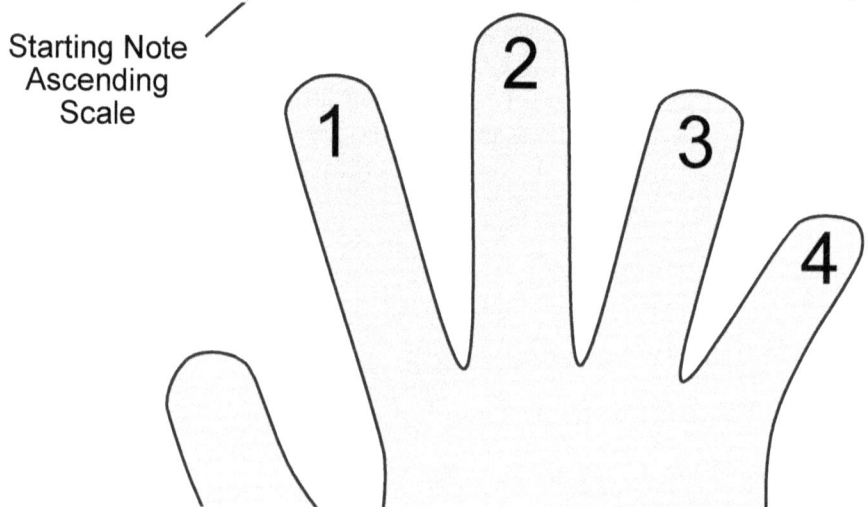

This is the same pattern starting on the A string:

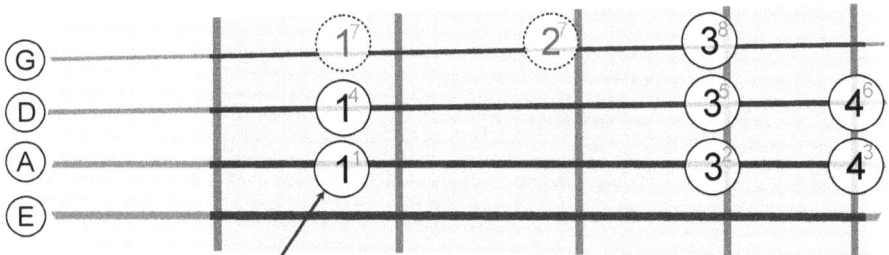

N.B. The frets are not numbered because this pattern can start on any fret on the E or A string.

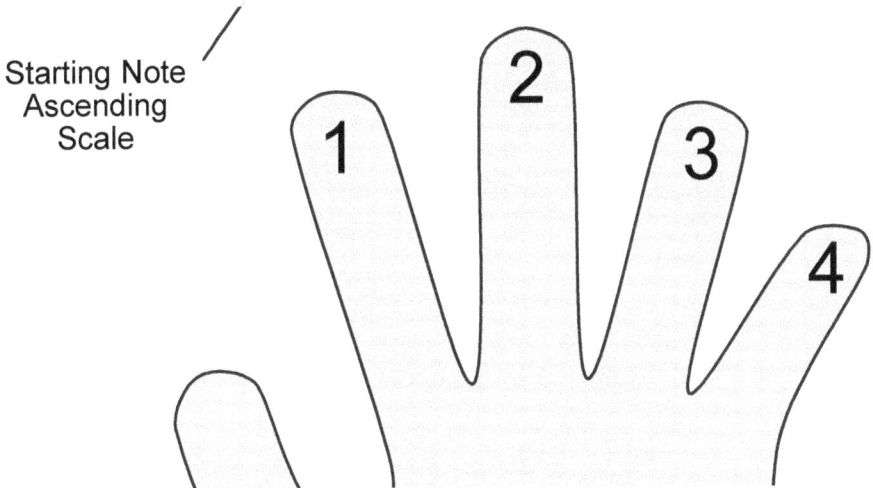

Starting Note Ascending Scale

Just as with the major scale, playing with one finger per fret may feel like a big stretch and the little finger may feel very awkward to start with, however, this is a skill worth persevering with. It will make it easier to navigate the fretboard, create bass parts and improvise solos. Also, being able to use all four fingers greatly increases playing speed and dramatically reduces the amount the bassist needs to move up and down the fretboard.

The frets at the higher end on the bass are closer together. If you are struggling with the stretches, start the scale on the A string further down the fretboard and work back towards the head as your hands get used to this new position.

Common Intervals

In western music, intervals between notes are referred to in relation to their position in the major and minor scales. For example: a fourth is the distance between the first and fourth degree of the scale and the fifth is the distance between the first and fifth degree. Where there is a difference between the interval in the major and minor scale, there is both a major and minor interval. For example, the major third is derived from the major scale and the minor third from the minor scale.

Knowing and finding intervals on the bass guitar is another really important way to navigate the fretboard. Below are diagrams of seven common intervals: minor third, major third, fourth, fifth, minor sixth, major sixth and an octave (an eighth or the next occurrence of the first). The interval is shown both along the string and across the strings. None of the diagrams include fret numbers because the interval is the same whatever fret or string you start on. You can use the scales to find any other intervals you want.

Minor 3rd
Movement: forward 3 frets

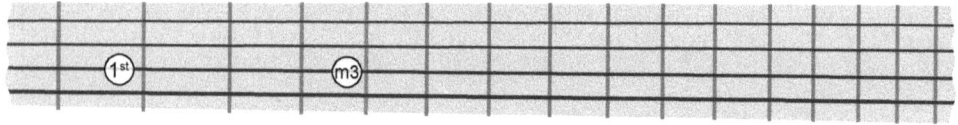

Movement: up 1 string and back 2 frets

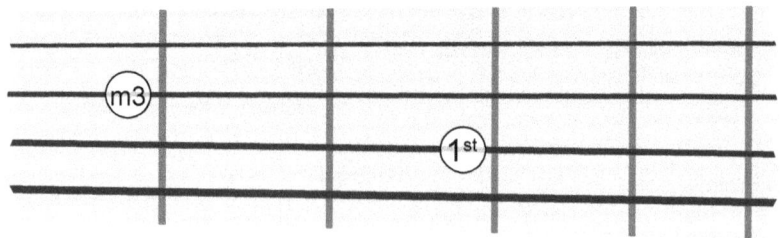

Major 3rd
Movement: forward 4 frets

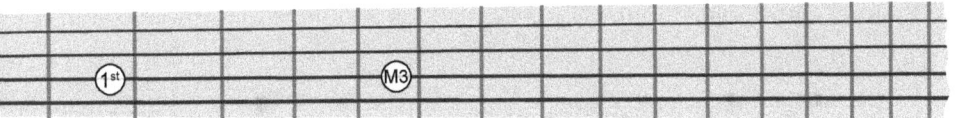

Movement: up 1 string and back 1 fret

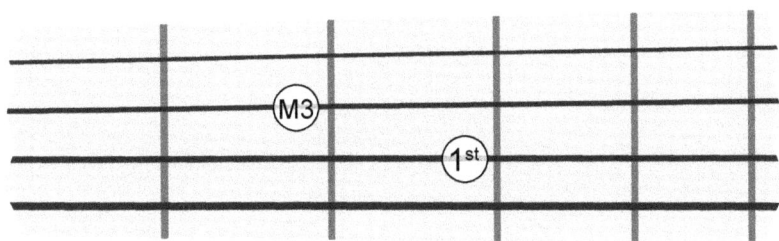

4th
Movement: forward 5 frets

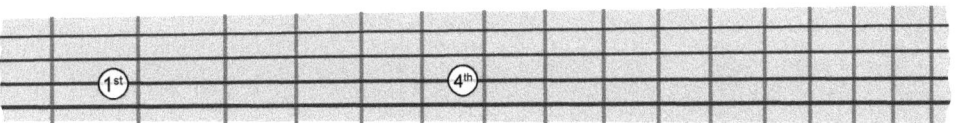

Movement: directly up 1 string

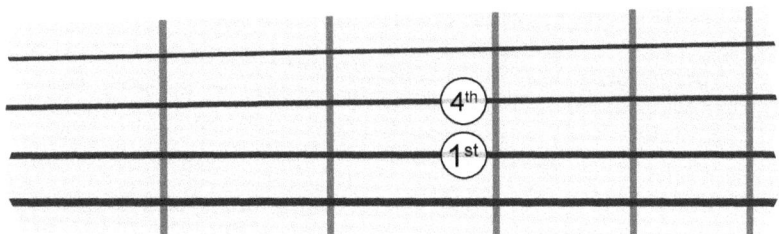

5th
Movement: forward 7 frets

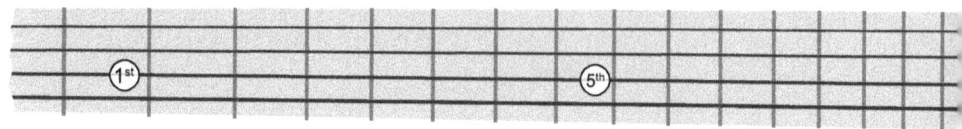

Movement: up 1 string and forward 2 frets

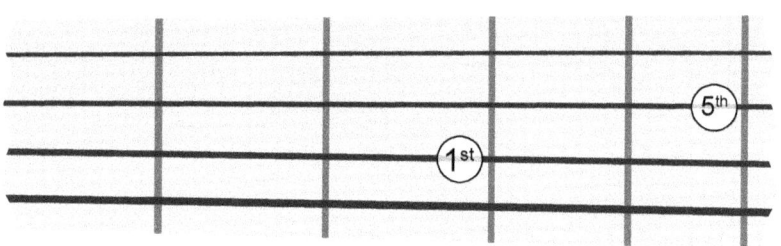

Minor 6th
Movement: forward 8 frets

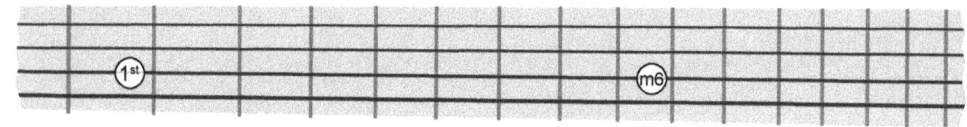

Movement: up 1 string and forward 3 frets

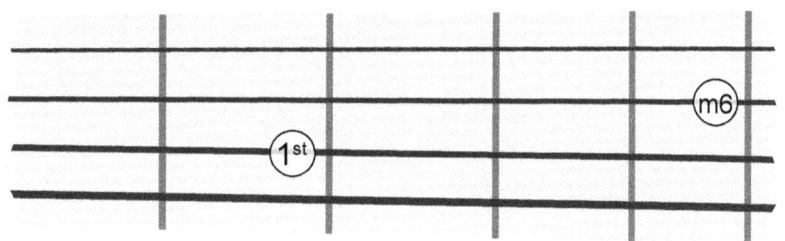

Major 6th
Movement: forward 9 frets

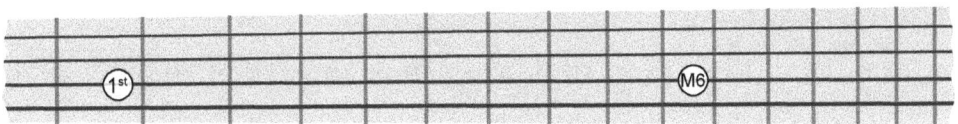

Movement: up 2 strings and back 1 fret

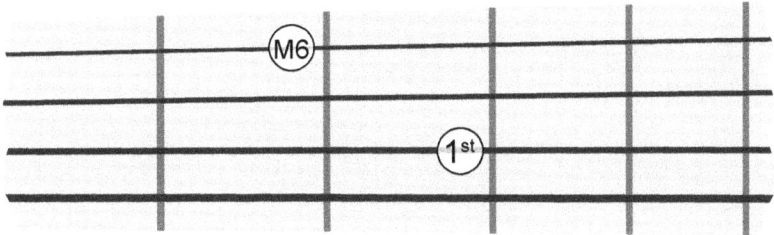

The Octave (8th)

The octave is the most important interval to know because it is always the starting point of the next scale pattern in the same key. If you move up an octave you can use the same patterns and intervals from this new starting point.

Octave (8th)
Movement: forward 12 frets

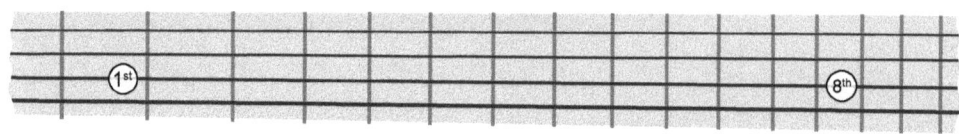

Movement: up 1 string and forward 7 frets

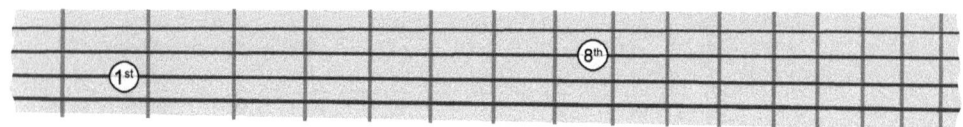

Movement: up 2 strings and forward 2 frets

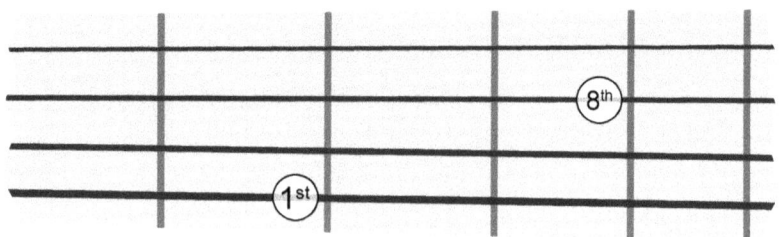

Common Chords and How to Find Them

Chords are made up of three or more notes played together. Chords within a key are numbered according to their position in the scale. The most common chords are Chords I, IV, V and VI and many songs use only these chords. When using a scale pattern it is easy to find the bass notes for these (and other) chords by knowing these positions within the scale. You can easily create moving bass parts by using other notes from the scale to move between the bass notes of the chords.

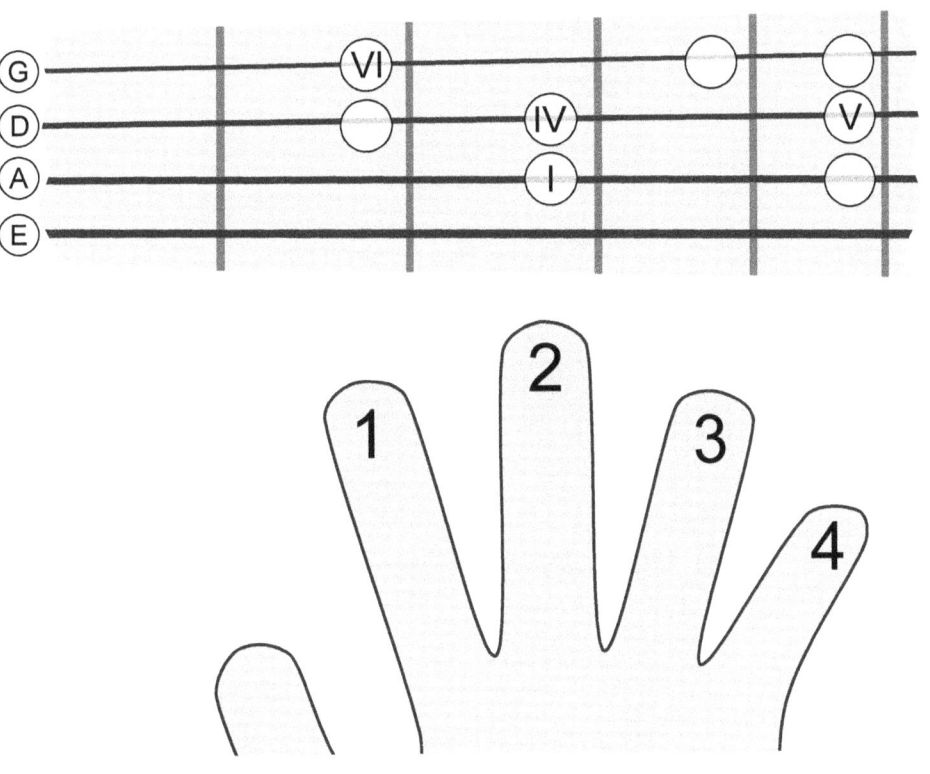

Notes Within a Chord

Common chords consists of the bass note of the chord and the third and fifth intervals above it in the key you are playing. For example: Chord IV uses the 4th note of the scale as its bass note and and the third and fifth intervals above it which are the 6th and 8th degrees of the scale.

The bass note is known as the root of the chord. When creating a bass part, playing the root of the chord, when the chord begins creates a strong sound. However, when a different feel is desired, a different note from the chord may be used as the bass note and this is called an inversion. When an inversion is desired, it is written as the 'chord/bass note'. For example, G/B where G is the chord but B is the lowest note played. Using an inversion changes the feel of the music.

Below are diagrams representing the notes making up a major and minor chords. The three notes within the chord are referred to as the 1^{st}(root), 3rd and 5th.

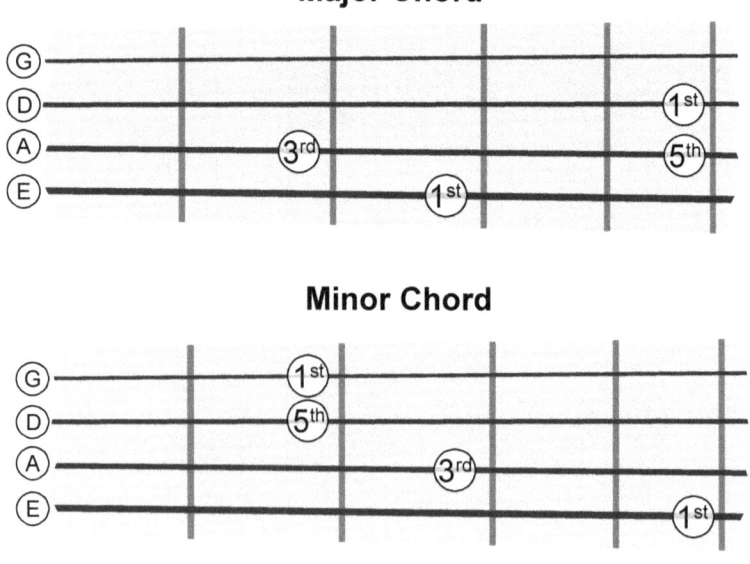

These are the four most common chords. The scale pattern has been extended to show the placement of higher and lower notes within the chord.

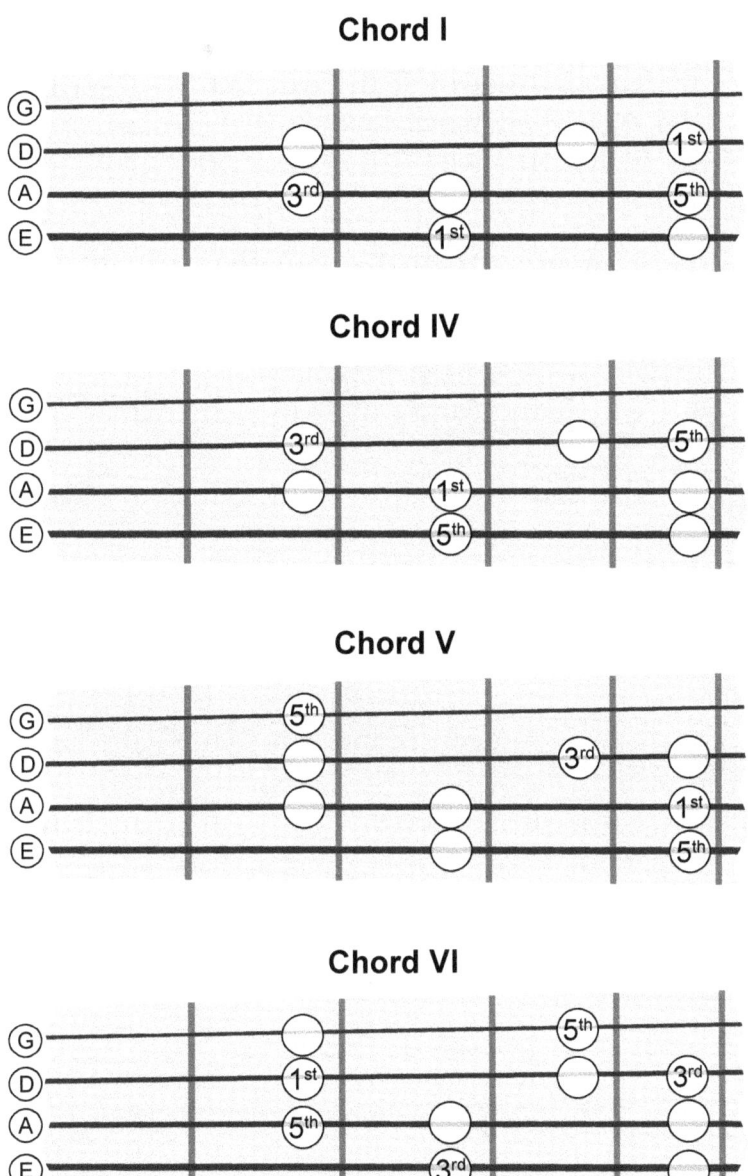

The Pentatonic Scale

A pentatonic scale is any scale consisting of five repeating notes rather than seven as used in the major and minor scales. Pentatonic scales form the basis of music from all around the world including much modern pop, rock and funk. The most useful pentatonic scale for the bassist is the minor pentatonic. It fits easily under the hand and provides a solid foundation to work from and adapt, to give whatever feel you are looking for.

A minor pentatonic scale

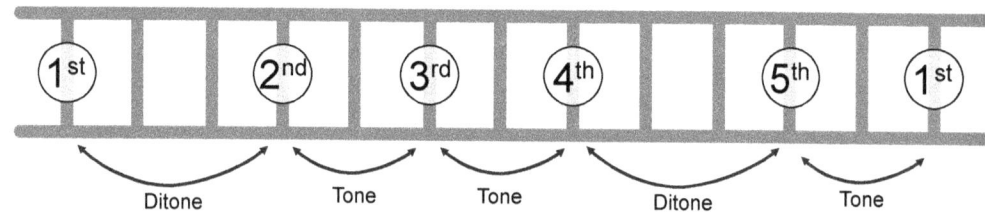

This translates onto the bass along the string as:

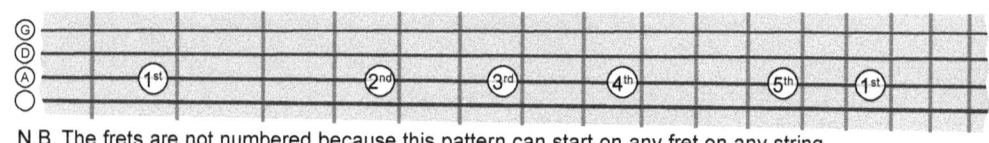

N.B. The frets are not numbered because this pattern can start on any fret on any string.

and translates across the strings as:

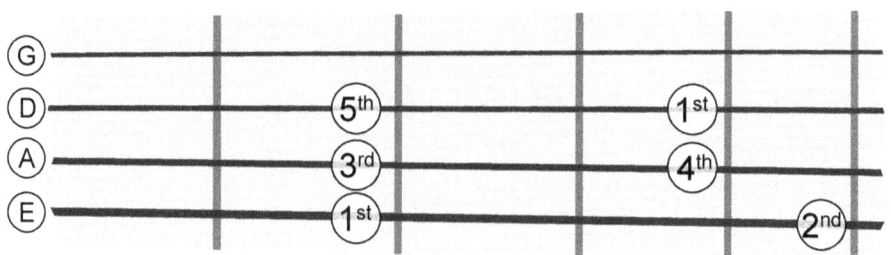

N.B. The frets are not numbered because this pattern can start on any fret on the E or A string.

Blues Notes & Passing Notes

Blues notes and passing notes are notes which are not a part of the original key or scale but which can be added to bring 'flavour' to the music.

The minor pentatonic scale provides a great framework for the bassist to work from. It allows the bassist to navigate around the fretboard. Adapting the scale by adding passing notes or blues notes makes it a really versatile pattern and allows the bassist to get the sound they desire. Just as with the other scales, the minor pentatonic scale pattern should be treated as a guide and not a rule. You can adapt this scale in anyway you like, raising and lowering notes or adding 'passing' notes between the 'fixed' notes to aid the movement of the bass part. There are two 'passing' notes that are extremely useful toward getting a truly funky sound. I have added these onto the fretboard diagram as 'P' for passing. You can, of course, use them in anyway you like.

and translates across the strings as:

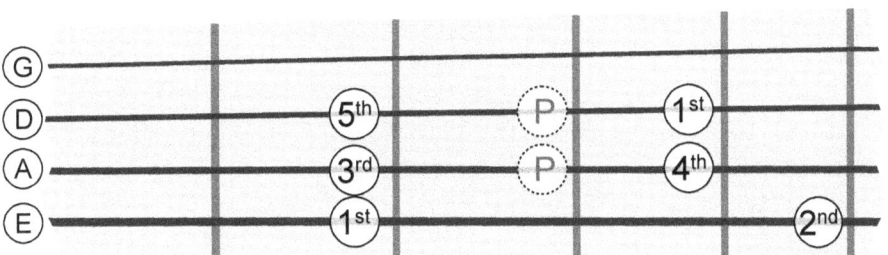

N.B. The frets are not numbered because this pattern can start on any fret on the E or A string.

This is a fun scale to play and experiment with. It is extremely versatile and fun and provides a route map to enable you to move around the fretboard of the bass, creating parts and improvising; giving freedom to the bassist. Remember, when experimenting with this scale there are no wrong notes, just some notes which sound better than others. Add in your own passing notes and see what sounds you can get!

Playing The Minor Pentatonic Scale

To play the minor pentatonic scale, select a fret on either the E or A string and place your first finger on it. The note of this fret is the key of the scale. For example, starting with the first finger on the seventh fret of the E string produces the note B and the scale of B pentatonic minor.

The diagram below shows the scale pattern with fingering numbers. Position your hand around the chosen fret and imagine a block of four frets with one per finger. Play the ascending scale by starting with the lowest string and playing left to right from the lowest note to the highest note along the string before moving up to the next string and doing the same. The descending scale starts with the highest note and works downward, right to left before moving down a string and continuing right to left. Notes of the scale are numbered in superscript above the fingering number.

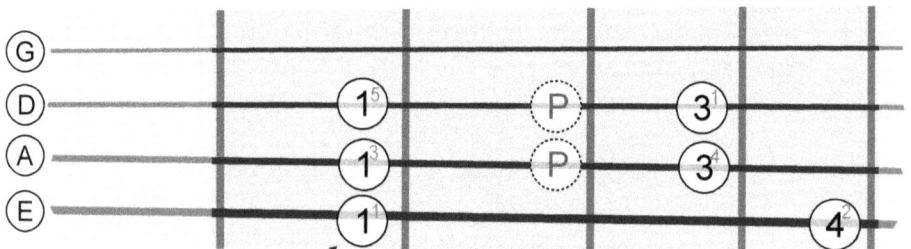

N.B. The frets are not numbered because this pattern can start on any fret on the E or A string.

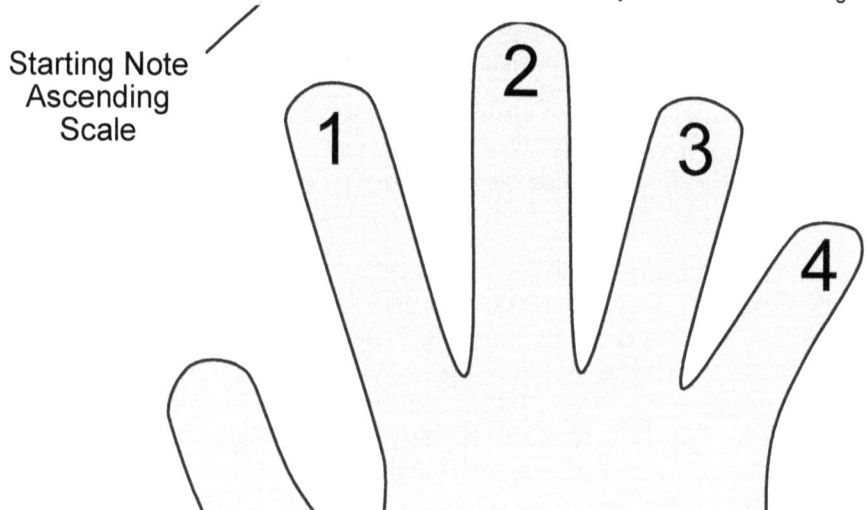

Starting Note Ascending Scale

This is the same pattern starting on the A string

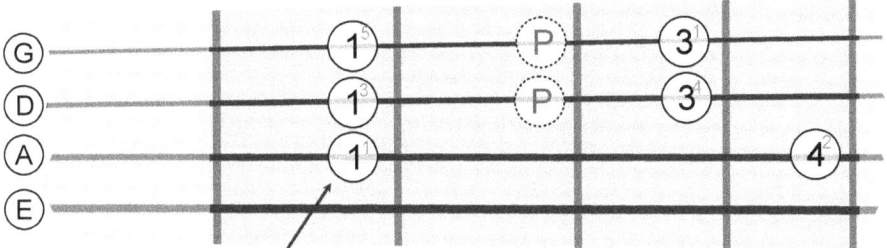

N.B. The frets are not numbered because this pattern can start on any fret on the E or A string.

Starting Note Ascending Scale

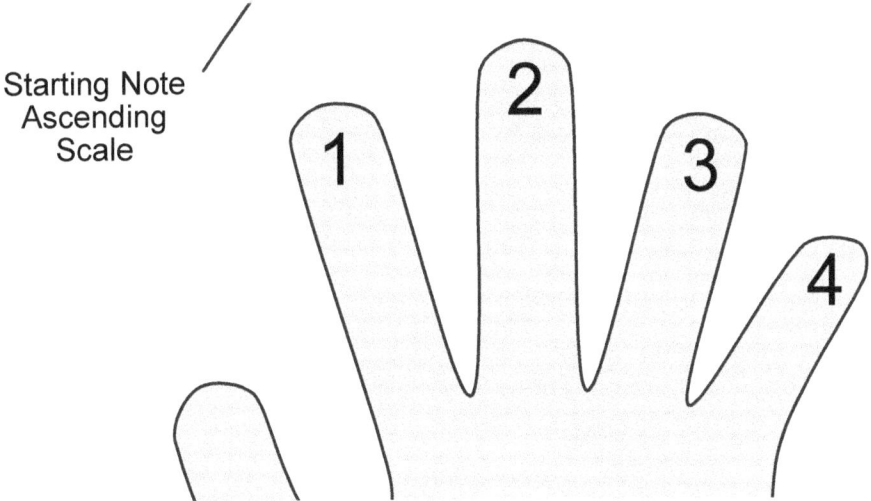

Just as with the major scale, playing with one finger per fret may feel like a big stretch and the little finger may feel very awkward to start with, however, this is a skill worth persevering with. It will make it easier to navigate the fretboard, create bass parts and improvise solos. Also, being able to use all four fingers greatly increases playing speed and dramatically reduces the amount the bassist needs to move up and down the fretboard to find notes.

The frets at the higher end on the bass are closer together. If you are struggling with the stretches, start the scale on the A string further down the fretboard and work back towards the head as your hands get used to this new position.

The Blues Scale

The blues scale is an adaption of the major scale where the seventh note is flattened but, like the pentatonic scale, it only regularly uses five notes. As with the other scales, it can also start on any note (naturals, sharps or flats).

A major scale - tone and semitone pattern

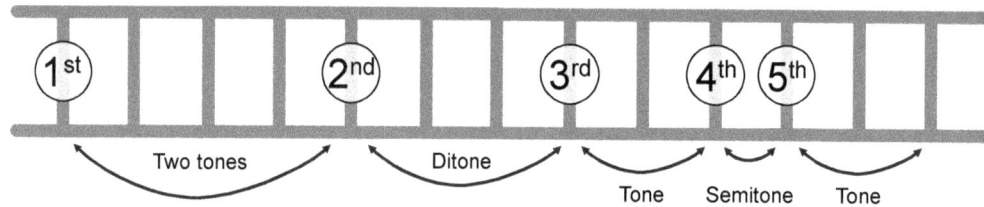

This translates onto the bass along the string as:

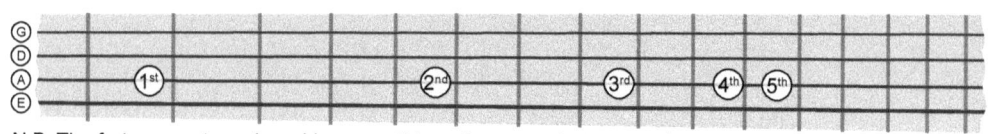

N.B. The frets are not numbered because this pattern can start on any fret on any string.

and translates across the strings as:

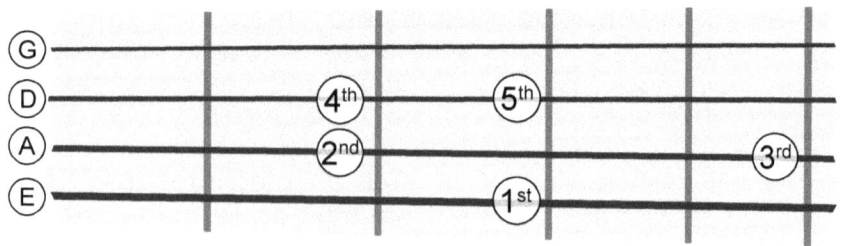

N.B. The frets are not numbered because this pattern can start on any fret on the E or A string.

Playing The Blues Scale

To play the blues scale, select a fret on either the E or the A string and place your second finger on it. The note of this fret is the key of the scale. In a 12 Bar Blues the scale is used first starting on the E string and then again on the A string so it is good to get used to playing this scale starting from either string.

The diagram below shows the scale pattern with fingering numbers. Position your hand around the chosen fret and imagine a block of four frets, one per finger. Play the ascending scale by starting with the lowest string and playing left to right along the string before moving up to the next string. The descending scale starts with the highest note and works downward, right to left before moving down a string and continuing right to left. Notes of the scale are numbered in superscript above the fingering number.

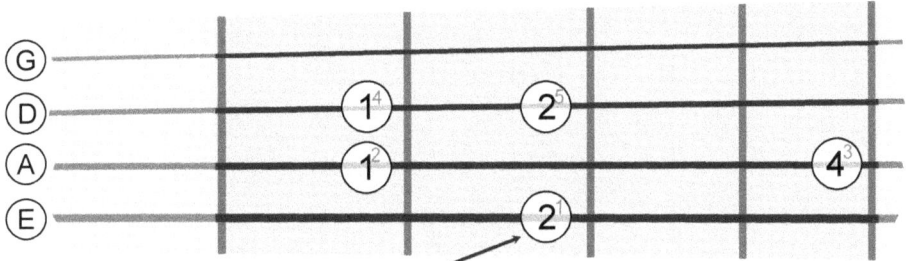

N.B. The frets are not numbered because this pattern can start on any fret on the E or A string.

Starting Note
Ascending
Scale

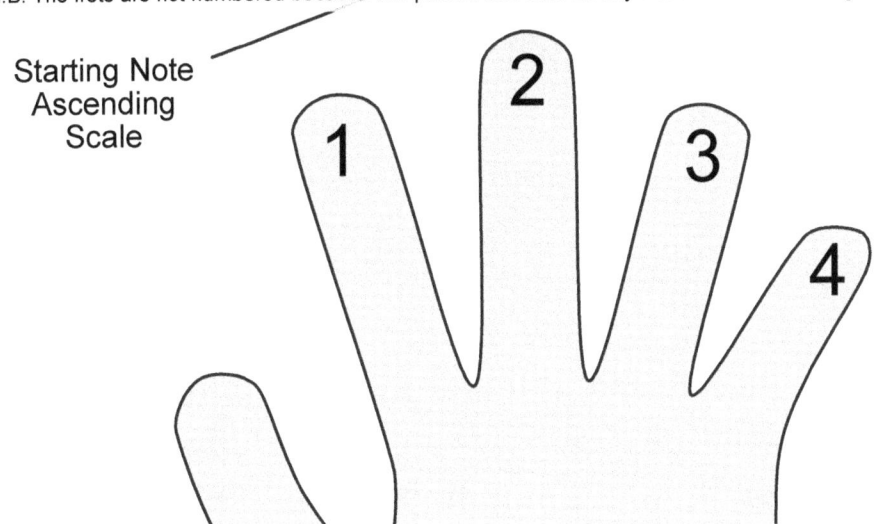

TAB

TAB

TAB

TAB

TAB

TAB

TAB

TAB

T			
A			
B			

T			
A			
B			

T			
A			
B			

T			
A			
B			

T			
A			
B			

T			
A			
B			

TAB

TAB

Numerical by scale

Scale Type: _____

Numerical by scale

Scale Type: _____

Numerical by scale

Scale Type: _____

Numerical by scale

Scale Type: _____

Numerical by scale

Scale Type: _____

Numerical by scale

Scale Type: _____

Numerical by scale

Scale Type: _____

Numerical by scale

Scale Type: _____

Numerical by scale

Scale Type: _____

Numerical by scale

Scale Type: _____

Notes

Notes

Notes

Notes

Notes

Notes

Notes

Notes

Notes

Notes

www.ingramcontent.com/pod-product-compliance
Lightning Source LLC
Chambersburg PA
CBHW041150110526
44590CB00027B/4180